IF YOU START A FIRE [BE PREPARED TO BURN]

Kevin Kautzman

BROADWAY PLAY PUBLISHING INC
New York
www.broadwayplaypublishing.com
info@broadwayplaypublishing.com

IF YOU START A FIRE [BE PREPARED TO BURN]
© Copyright 2021 Kevin Kautzman

First edition: March 2021
I S B N: 978-0-88145-899-2

Book design: Marie Donovan
Page make-up: Adobe InDesign
Typeface: Palatino

IF YOU START A FIRE [BE PREPARED TO BURN] was written with the support of a 2009-10 Jerome Fellowship from the Playwrights' Center in Minneapolis and developed in part with support from a 2012 Seed Grant from ScriptWorks.

The play received its first staged reading in August of 2011 at the New Theatre Project in Ypsilanti, Michigan. It received readings in May and June of 2012 from Mondays Dark in New York and the Des Moines Social Club.

IF YOU START A FIRE [BE PREPARED TO BURN] was originally presented by the New Theatre Project (Artistic Director, Keith Paul Medalis) in Ypsilanti, Michigan, on 17 February 2012. The cast and creative contributors were:

CHRIS/CHRIXXX..Peter Giessl
LUCY/LUXXX ....Elise Randall
BIG_BEN *(voice)*.................................... Keith Paul Medalis
TOMMYKNOCKER *(voice)* ....Andrew Sandoval

Director... Natividad Salgado
Designs ....Janine Woods Thoma

IF YOU START A FIRE [BE PREPARED TO BURN] premiered in New York on 14 September 2012 at the 45th Street Theatre, produced by Mondays Dark (Executive Director, Rob Hinderliter; Artistic Director, Anthony Johnson; Managing Director Dominick LaRuffa Jr). The cast and creative contributors were:

CHRIS/CHRIXXX.................................... Lenny Platt
LUCY/LUXXX .... Spencer Rose
BIG_BEN & TOMMYKNOCKER *(voice)* .... Ryan Krause
BIG_BEN & TOMMYKNOCKER *(shadow)* .... Jade Ziane

Director .... Kenny Howard
A/V .... Terence Krey
Costumes .... Joshua McKinley
Lighting .... Spencer Bazzano & Brian McManimon
Photography .... Dwayne Williams
Props & dressing .... Rebecca Fisher
Scenic design .... Jessica Moretti
Technical direction .... Thom Caska
Interns .... Vincent Cinque, Avery Dresel Kurtz,
                        Austin Klich & Madeline White

CHARACTERS & SETTING

LUCY / LUXXX, *F, 20s*
CHRIS / CHRIXXX, *M, 20s*
BIG_BEN, *a client*
TOMMYKNOCKER, *a client*

A note on casting: the play requires a cast of two or three, depending on how you intend to handle BIG_BEN *and* TOMMYKNOCKER.

CHRIS *and* LUCY's *apartment. The Epilogue takes place in their starter mansion.*

SCENES

NOTES ON THE SCRIPT

A dash at the end of a line (—) suggests a hard interruption. The character who speaks next should sharply interrupt the character delivering the dashed line.

A slash at the end of a line (/) suggests a soft interruption. The character who speaks next should begin his or her line early such that both characters speak briefly at the same time.

[Text in brackets happens via chat.] To represent this, a projector or displays might be used in combination with voice over. Feel free to find what works for you so long as you don't require the audience to read what happens in chat, as I imagine this would probably become tedious.

The New Theatre Project used voiceovers and thirteen salvaged computer monitors on which the video chat appeared. It was not possible to read the chat on these monitors, though they did give the impression that a chat was taking place. This was effective when combined with voiceovers, the idea being that the voices are what CHRIS and LUCY hear in their minds while reading the chat. I also think it could be very satisfying to cast a third actor to read the chat parts live.

In Mondays Dark's New York premiere at the 45th Street Theatre, no screens were used or images projected. Instead a third actor appeared in shadow within a rectangular frame above the stage, accompanied by voiceovers. This was an effective way to make BIG_BEN's and TOMMYKNOCKER's presences felt while keeping them anonymous. They were differentiated by different colored light, and TOMMYKNOCKER wore a hat.

Bottom line, this is a script that can be produced with a lot or little tech. Just find what works best for your company.

Goethe said, "Talent is developed in privacy",
you know? And it's really true. There is a need for
aloneness which I don't think most people realize for
an actor. It's almost having certain kinds of secrets for
yourself that you'll let the whole world in on only for a
moment, when you're acting.
Marilyn Monroe

Boy meets girl, so what?
Brecht

ACT ONE
AmericaInHeat.com

Scene 1
A PLANT FOR HANGING

(CHRIS *and* LUCY'S *apartment. She sits at the dining table with a textbook and laptop. She types at the laptop. There is a plain box upon the table across from her.*)

(CHRIS *enters. He wears the uniform of the trucking company for which he drives. He removes the baseball cap with the company's logo and throws it to the side. He goes to the kitchen and returns with a six pack of beer. He guzzles one and starts on a second.*)

CHRIS: What's this?

LUCY: It's a hanging plant.

(CHRIS *pulls a plant from within the box.*)

LUCY: It's a plant for hanging.

CHRIS: Where are we going to hang it?

LUCY: I thought maybe the office.

CHRIS: What office?

LUCY: That general area. Use your imagination. How was your day?

CHRIS: Awful. Yours?

LUCY: Same. My feet hurt. I miss you. We never see each other. I have to do this, though. Otherwise I wait tables forever. Or get some kind of degrading, pseudo job. And I don't want to be a secretary. A temp. A coordinator. A coordinating consultant. A consulting coordinator. A substitute teacher. An actual teacher. A tutor. I don't want any job that begins with a T.

CHRIS: Tank-operator.

LUCY: Definitely not.

CHRIS: You'd be a terrible tank-operator.

LUCY: It's just three years. Then I'll have my M B A. I'll get a good job with benefits. Maybe I can telecommute. People will finally start to respect me! And if not, we'll just buy some respect. And free time. We'll find new hobbies! Expensive, sporty hobbies! Maybe I'll golf!

CHRIS: Golf?

LUCY: Golf. Or ski!

CHRIS: You hate the cold.

LUCY: I'll buy a jacket! What the sport is doesn't matter. The point is to take up an activity that costs a lot and talk about it a bunch. It's a tactful way to tell people you've got money and free time. That way they know you're a first class citizen and treat you accordingly!

CHRIS: Golf?

LUCY: Why not?

CHRIS: What am I going to do while you're golfing?

LUCY: You can stop driving that truck. Maybe go back to school…

CHRIS: Sure. I can get an English degree. Wait tables. Operate tanks.

LUCY: At least I finished.

CHRIS: I'm sorry. Today was shit. They made me run half of Thompson's route. I'm exhausted. I hate driving that truck.

LUCY: My day wasn't a peach either, thanks for asking. I had this one asshole… oh excuse me "guest"… who actually grabbed my ass.

CHRIS: Bastard.

LUCY: I told Jonathan, but he didn't do anything! It was during lunch, and we were slammed. Some vacuum convention or something.

CHRIS: That sucks. Ahh. Ha? Ha…

LUCY: Ha ha ha. Vacuums do suck! Turns out the guy's a "friend" of the "Regional Manager." "Oh, Lucy. I'm sure he didn't mean it. He's on his second Manhattan."

(CHRIS *touches* LUCY *suggestively. Her response lives somewhere between reluctant and hungry.*)

CHRIS: You should have done something.

LUCY: You know what thought went through my head? It's my period, right?

CHRIS: *(Standing off)* I pay strict attention to your cycle.

LUCY: Don't be sarcastic.

CHRIS: I'm not! You leave all these implements in the bathroom. Some days I go in there and I don't know what's happened. It's like a snake after it molts!

LUCY: I wanted to take out my tampon and dip it in his third Manhattan.

CHRIS: That's disgusting.

LUCY: I seriously considered it. The worst thing I could do to him without him really knowing.

CHRIS: Who are you?

LUCY: Oh come on. He probably has a tampon fetish. Probably sticks them in his nostrils at night, adds a little water, and breathes through his mouth. Imagines he's sailing or something.

CHRIS: When do you have time to come up with these things?

LUCY: Waitresses harbor a lot of rage. Rage turns into thoughts. Weird thoughts. Anyway, that guy was a royal douche. Look what you did. Now I can't focus.

CHRIS: It's part of the job, isn't it? Guys get a little drunk and grab waitresses on the ass. It's like a rite of passage. Hazing. We're just monkeys, right? What? Don't look at me like that! Oh come on. I went to a good liberal arts college just like you. At least I had the brains to quit before they took all the money I didn't have to begin with. I'm so absolutely a feminist!

LUCY: Get me a beer then, Mister Feminist.

(CHRIS *gets* LUCY *a beer and makes a show of opening it for her. She slaps his ass.*)

LUCY: See, that doesn't bother me.

(CHRIS, *turns on her, pawing.*)

LUCY: This is a different context. Ahh! Get away from me. You stink.

CHRIS: *(Pouting, touching the plant)* Where am I supposed to hang this?

LUCY: Over the wireless router?

CHRIS: I'll do it tomorrow. Gah! Look at all these bills. I've got a new name for our generation: Generation Fucked. You like it? It's either that or "the Recession Generation," and I think "Generation Fucked" is better. It's got a lot of punch.

LUCY: You're very creative.

CHRIS: Bill. Past due bill. Hey! Coupons for shit we don't need! Bill. Bill. Bill.

LUCY: Welcome to the new normal.

CHRIS: I'm sick of living check to check. We're just treading water.

LUCY: It's better than drowning.

CHRIS: What are you working on?

LUCY: I have to do a presentation. Ugh.

CHRIS: Hey! Flex those poetry muscles. Recite some verse for me. No? Fine. Hey, you should write your presentation in verse!
And lo, in the third quarter of the fifth fiscal year of our Lord Money Verily the trumpets Flowery love will blow/

LUCY: Don't mock me.

CHRIS: You're the published poet.

LUCY: One poem in *Angry Feminists: A Bitch Journal.* It's not a serious publication.

CHRIS: It's on the shelf, isn't it?
What are you doing?

(LUCY *looks up from the computer.*)

CHRIS: I'm bonding with our new plant. We're watching you work.
(*Voicing the plant and wiggling it: a leafy puppet*)
Hello, Lucy! I'm a Hanging Plant. Feed me! Touch me! Love me!

(LUCY *stares at* CHRIS.)

LUCY: Are you done?

CHRIS: Umm. Yeah. So what's the presentation?

LUCY: I have to write a business plan.

CHRIS: Can you write a plan in which we are reborn into rich families?

LUCY: It doesn't work that way.

CHRIS: The golden rule: the folks with the gold—

CHRIS & LUCY: Make the rules.

CHRIS: I just wished they'd share a little more. Spread it around.

LUCY: I'm sure they wished you'd work harder for less.

CHRIS: (*Grabbing her laptop*) Seems like they've figured out how to do that. Seems like they let the leash out just enough so we get confident, then they yank the thing back and we all behave again. We grovel and hope they let the leash out like they used to, and by the time they do, we've forgotten there's a leash. Wash, rinse, repeat.

LUCY: That sounds right. What are you going to do about it?
(*She takes the laptop.*)
I'm going to work on this. I'd like to join their ranks, you know? I'd settle on becoming an assistant to a priest in the capitalist hierarchy. All I want is to sell out if they'd only just let me! I'll carry laundry for a rich misogynist if it means a salary with benefits. Health insurance. Dental insurance. 401k…maternity leave. I mean, the benefits from your job are okay, but they're not great. Sorry. It's true. I know we should have perspective. At least your job insures us.

(CHRIS *stands and takes off his shirt. He takes off his pants. He stands in his boxers. He opens a window.* LUCY *taps at the keyboard. He stands there.*)

CHRIS: (*Exiting to the kitchen*) I lost my job.

LUCY: What?!

CHRIS: (*Off*) Welcome to the new normal!

LUCY: What are you doing?!

CHRIS: (*Off*) Setting my uniform on fire!

LUCY: Not in the house!

CHRIS: *(Off)* It's not a house! It's an apartment!
(He enters, still wearing only his boxers. He holds a smoking cooking pot in his hands, which are covered with oven mitts.)
Quick quick quick! Open the door!

LUCY: You're insane!

CHRIS: The door, Lucy!

(LUCY opens the door. CHRIS streaks out with the smoking pot only to return a few moments later.)

LUCY: What the hell is wrong with you!?

CHRIS: I didn't like that job anyway.

LUCY: We can't survive off my tips, and I can't do any more shifts. I have to focus on the M B A!

CHRIS: Maybe if you smile when guys grab you, you'll get bigger tips. Then we're really living!

LUCY: What the hell happened?

CHRIS: I did most of Thompson's route today on top of my own, and he didn't even say "thank you". He was at the bar right at five watching the game. He'd been faking sick, and he laughed at me. You know how Thompson laughs. Hurr hurr hurr. So I fucking punched him.

LUCY: You punched him for his laugh?

CHRIS: I would have punched his laugh if it was punchable, but it's not, so I punched the place from whence the laugh originates: his face.

LUCY: You have to apologize.

CHRIS: I'm sick of groveling.

LUCY: What if they press charges?

CHRIS: They won't. Thompson kind of pushed me first. There were words. It's complicated. You'll be glad to know I was technically laid off, not fired.

That company isn't exactly on the level. And I think Thompson's known for years.

LUCY: Known what?

CHRIS: Their books are cooked. Somebody's fucking somebody and not wearing protection. The fuckee doesn't even know he's the fuckee, which is the worst way to get fucked! The fucker sure knows there's fucking going on, though. Woo boy. And I think I know who the fucker is. I think the fucker's/

LUCY: Don't tell me! La la la la la la la la la!

CHRIS: But I know who the fucker is!

LUCY: You're a criminal mastermind. What's your point?

CHRIS: They're not going to challenge my unemployment. We're not going to starve.

LUCY: Chris, dear, did you blackmail your employer?

CHRIS: Ex-employer. And no. They offered. Why would I lie? It's going to be fine.

LUCY: Oh good! Fine. You only lost a job with benefits in the worst job market since Prohibition!

CHRIS: Good point! Let's toast the end of Prohibition. No?

LUCY: We were going to buy a house!

CHRIS: I know!

LUCY: Weren't we friends with Thompson?

CHRIS: He had it coming.

LUCY: Typical! You acted out, and now we're screwed. What if one of us gets sick?

CHRIS: We'll take cough medicine and drink chamomile tea.

LUCY: No! Sick like really sick! Sick like we get an arm cut off! We're running around armless!

CHRIS: How are we going to lose an arm?

LUCY: These things happen! We'll go into the hospital, they'll cauterize the stump, send us the bill to end all bills, and we'll lose everything!

CHRIS: What everything?

(CHRIS *and* LUCY *look around their apartment. They have little to lose except perhaps some credit debt, outdated consumer electronics, secondhand furniture, a half-read copy of* Angry Feminist: A Bitch Journal, *and a plant for hanging.*)

LUCY: I don't want to lose my arm.

CHRIS: Your arm isn't going to fall off. We're fine. We're fit, young specimens. Look at us!

(CHRIS *beats his chest and shows off his various parts. He is indeed well assembled. He pulls* LUCY'S *arm and shows her to herself.*)

LUCY: What are we going to do?

CHRIS: I have two years of college.

LUCY: Oh yeah. What did you study? Oh that's right. Hallucinogenic drugs!

CHRIS: And Philosophy! And Latin!

LUCY: Great! Call Rome and ask them when we can expect universal health care and a robust job market! Latin! Why Latin?

CHRIS: I like the way it sounds! Salve. Vale. In nomine Patris. Et cetera. Et not eck. I hate when people say "eck." Et et et. I'm educated! Et et et cetera!

LUCY: You need to find another job.

CHRIS: What's the rush? I get unemployment. It's free money!

LUCY: Unemployment doesn't mean security. It means we can't even begin to think about having a family/

(CHRIS *shows his hand to* LUCY.)

CHRIS: Look at this.

LUCY: Don't change the subject!

CHRIS: I'm wounded.

LUCY: Are those teeth marks?

CHRIS: Mmhmm.

LUCY: Did Thompson bite you?

CHRIS: Mmhmm.

LUCY: Before or after you punched him?

CHRIS: Does it matter?

LUCY: Yes!

CHRIS: After.

LUCY: *(Exiting)* Did you disinfect it?

CHRIS: No.

LUCY: *(Off)* We don't have any peroxide.

CHRIS: We have vodka.

(LUCY *returns with vodka and a towel.*)

LUCY: Human mouths are filthy.

CHRIS: Look at you. You'd be a great, sexy nurse. Rarr.

LUCY: Don't even try your lame moves on me. Jobless deadbeats don't get sympathy sex. This is going to sting.

CHRIS: Ow.

LUCY: You smell. Blah. Punching Thompson. You deserved to get bit. I'm really angry at you.

CHRIS: You aren't acting angry.

LUCY: Oh but I am! I am angry at you! Rarr. Snarl. Anger. Anger!

CHRIS: It's going to be okay.

LUCY: I will not be in one of those relationships where you stay at home and fiddle on your guitar in your stained underwear while I get my butt grabbed ten hours a day for extra big tips. I left home to get away from people like that.

CHRIS: Why don't we start a business? There are all kinds of initiatives for small businesses. We're small. We just need to get busy. Then we'll be a small business.

LUCY: It's not that easy. It takes capital. And you need an idea.

CHRIS: No you don't! Plenty of idiots are rich. You don't need an idea to make money. You need straight teeth and something to sell.

LUCY: All right, genius. Our teeth are straight. What do we have to sell?

CHRIS: We don't really own anything. Just clothes and a couple computers.

LUCY: You could always long haul.

CHRIS: No way! That shit killed my uncle!

LUCY: I thought he overdosed on coke.

CHRIS: Which he took to stay awake and drive the truck!

LUCY: They're always hiring! I see signs on the trucks. "We're hiring!"

CHRIS: No. I can't do it. I can barely hold down a local route. I wouldn't survive out there. I would lose my mind one night between Dubuque and Kansas City and drive ninety miles into a ditch. You'd get a call at three AM from some highway patrolman saying they found me stark naked with the words "4 REAL" cut into my arm and an ounce of coke up my ass. The patrolman will say, "It's the cocaine that killed him. When his sphincter tightened from the crash the bag burst and, well, there's only so much cocaine the human body can tolerate all at once. I'm very sorry. When we found him he was still alive. He kept saying, 'Pass the salad. Pass the salad. Pass the salad.' Does that mean anything to you, Miss?" And it won't mean anything to you, because it's nonsense. And you'll cry and cry and never eat a salad again. Is that what you want? Never to eat salad!?

LUCY: They make good money is all.

CHRIS: So do strippers.

LUCY: Do they get benefits?

CHRIS: Stripping?

LUCY: I'll strip if I want to strip!

CHRIS: You want to strip?

LUCY: No.

CHRIS: We need something to sell.

LUCY: We don't have anything.

CHRIS: We have something. We have you. You're gorgeous.

LUCY: You're not bad looking yourself. For a jobless deadbeat.

CHRIS: I bet tons of people would want a piece of what we have. You've been told you could model!

LUCY: Years ago. By my mom.

CHRIS: Strangers too!

LUCY: Guys trying to get into my pants.

CHRIS: Why don't we sell that?

LUCY: Sell what?

CHRIS: Sell you.

LUCY: Wait. You mean like sex?

CHRIS: Yes! But not actually sex. We sell the idea of you.

LUCY: I'm not a whore.

CHRIS: I'm not saying you're a whore. Exactly the opposite! You're a young, beautiful, intelligent woman. You turn heads!

LUCY: Thanks, honey. Why I'm with you is beyond me.

CHRIS: We're in love, remember?

LUCY: We can't sell me.

CHRIS: Why not? Look at this.
(He grabs her computer and turns on the webcam. He directs it at LUCY.)
Wave hello. See. They can see you. But they can't touch you. Ergo not a whore. Something else. The idea of a human. Post-human. They don't actually want a whore. They want something they can't touch or smell or taste. They want perfection!

LUCY: Who are "they"?

CHRIS: Visitors to your very own erotic website!

LUCY: Oh no no no no no!

CHRIS: People will pay just to look.

LUCY: No way. It's a terrible idea.
(She buries herself in her notebook.)

CHRIS: Yeah. You're probably right.
(He touches the plant with his good hand, making a show of thoughtfulness.)
I guess I'll take a shower then. Get ready for bed.

LUCY: Yeah, you'd better. Big day tomorrow. Have to get up and look for a job. Or are you going to sit in your boxers and play video games? Jerk off into a sock? Big man. Where I'm from we don't brag about collecting unemployment.

CHRIS: You can quit waiting tables. We'll work from home. Manage our own schedules. We'll take a holiday whenever we want. And nobody will touch you. You'll serve up an idea of yourself, and you'll get your life back in exchange. You will transcend your body. You'll be like an angel. A sex angel!

LUCY: You're serious.

CHRIS: We can get by on my unemployment while we launch a personal, insider website. It's all about the impression of access. And it has to be hot! That's what we'll call it! Hot... heat...something... America? Hot. Heat. America/

LUCY: America in Heat?

CHRIS: America in Heat dot com! It's perfect! Yeah. We take a set of still photos, do a teaser trailer, generate buzz, and sell a subscription for insider content and access to a live webcam and chat room. There are vast networks where people register to access adult content, and—

LUCY: How do you know all this? Okay. Right. Sorry I asked.

CHRIS: It is the twenty-first century! People don't live ethically! We can't. We can only live aesthetically! We live in a house of mirrors built on a house of cards built on a foundation of sand!

LUCY: Don't lecture me!

CHRIS: I'm not lecturing! I'm preaching! And I'm telling you there is freedom in hopelessness! God or whatever isn't going to descend from heaven and scold you because you show your tits and ass to strangers for money. This machine is powerful.

LUCY: It's just a fancy box.

CHRIS: It's a magic box! It can connect us to people with money who want what we have!

LUCY: What's that?

CHRIS: Youth. And beauty. And purity. Yeah. That's how we'll market you. You're the girl next door. Apple pie. A rainy day at the cabin. You're stranded and without firewood, but someone's at the door with some wood, and he's going to help keep you warm inside your blanket. Which is an American flag! Boom!

LUCY: You're serious.

CHRIS: Think about it. Nobody cares whether we have any dignity. Insurance. What happens if you get pregnant? We'd have to beg. And I don't want to beg. And I don't want to take out any more loans. They only care if you pay them to care. Socialism lost. Everything's for sale.

LUCY: How much do you think we could make?

CHRIS: A lot. You can build a cult, a umm…a fandom. When people subscribe to your website, you make money. Look at it like this: ten thousand people at ten dollars a year is a hundred thousand dollars. With that kind of money we could finally afford to stop renting. Buy a house. Start a family. You can golf!

LUCY: All that open space. So much green. I do actually kind of want to try it.

CHRIS: And if we succeed, you could.

LUCY: Could I buy a little hat?

CHRIS: Totally.

LUCY: I'd look good in one of those hats.

CHRIS: Yeah, you would.

Hey. I love you. Just think about it. Good night. Vale.

LUCY: Yeah. You too. Dork.

(CHRIS *exits.* LUCY *closes the textbook and looks at her computer. She hesitates. She types, searching for something. She finds it. Sex noises come from the device. She mutes it. She stares at the screen.)*

(End Scene)

Scene 2
OF THE LABIA

(A month later. CHRIS *and* LUCY's *apartment. The office area has been converted into a studio and now hosts a college-grade pull out couch of some garish color. There is a camera on a tripod. The potted plant remains on the dining table in the living area. They sit together on the couch, post-coital.)*

LUCY: That was kind of…

CHRIS: Fun?

LUCY: Degrading.

CHRIS: Degrading?

LUCY: And fun. Am I that damaged?

CHRIS: We feel safest when there's someone else in charge. Which is by definition degrading. We are graded down. Reduced. Broken—

LUCY: I get it.

The camera made me drunk. We haven't had sex like that since—

CHRIS: We first met.

LUCY: That was first-time sex.

CHRIS: More like third-time sex.

LUCY: Oh man, I love third-time sex.

CHRIS: Yeah.

LUCY: So many surprises. Like opening a—

CHRIS: Present. Yeah/

LUCY: Yeah. Ungh. Except you already know what's inside, and so you play with the wrapping. You tug at the bow a bit. I love that. Your fingers tracing a face. A chin. A neck.
Shoulders. Chest. Stomach.

CHRIS: Mmm. Pandora's fucking box, another human being. You never actually know what's gonna pop out.

LUCY: That's the fun part.

CHRIS: It's the scary part.

LUCY: It's the scary fun part. I'll be back.
(She exits toward the bathroom. Off)
How'd the photos turn out?

(CHRIS looks through the images.)

CHRIS: You are so hot in these!

LUCY: *(Off)* I know!

(CHRIS scratches himself. He yawns. He finds LUCY's bra on the floor. He tries it on awkwardly.)

LUCY: *(Returning)* What are you doing?

CHRIS: Trying on your bra.

LUCY: Oh my. So helpless. Like a newborn fawn.

CHRIS: I'm better at taking these off.

LUCY: You're an idiot. Here. Aww, that's precious.

CHRIS: How do I look?

LUCY: Like a man in a bra.

CHRIS: Don't get judgy.

(LUCY *snaps a few quick photos of* CHRIS.)

LUCY: Do something sexy.

(CHRIS *takes off the bra and ducks away.* LUCY *chases him with the camera.*)

CHRIS: Gimme!

LUCY: Can't take your own medicine?

CHRIS: Give me the camera!

LUCY: Let me take a picture of you with the bra!

CHRIS: No!

LUCY: Don't be a prude! I'm on that couch with my legs spread/

CHRIS: It's not the same!

LUCY: I have my legs spread so wide you can see my uterus!

CHRIS: I don't want that picture getting out!

LUCY: You practically shoved this camera inside me, and now you won't let me take one little picture!

CHRIS: We did it for the website! I don't want you to take a picture of me in your bra. Let's look at the pictures. Why do you want to take a picture of me in your bra?

LUCY: It'll make me feel better. Please?

CHRIS: Just don't send it to anybody.
(*He grabs the bra, attempts to put it on, and fails.*)

LUCY: Here. Let me help. Oh oh oh. Sit on the couch and arch your back. This is not optional. I spread my labia for you.

CHRIS: All right! Just don't say that word.

LUCY: What? Labia? Laaaaaaabia.

CHRIS: Eeeeeeeh. I don't like that word.

LUCY: It's Latin, isn't it? Arch your back.

CHRIS: Like this?

LUCY: Like that. Great! Very sexy. Very butch.

CHRIS: Butch?

(LUCY *takes a photo. Then another*)

CHRIS: Okay, okay. Enough.
(*He takes off the bra.*)

LUCY: Look! Ahh ha ha. That is priceless.

CHRIS: You can never show those to anybody.

LUCY: You've got a double standard, don't you?

CHRIS: Yours are for the website!

LUCY: The website. Yeah. Great. If my family ever sees these—

CHRIS: I like your family more than you do.

LUCY: That's because you weren't horribly damaged by them.

CHRIS: So why do you care?

LUCY: I just do. Ahh! Look at my mole!

CHRIS: The girl next door has moles!

LUCY: Not like that she doesn't. Ugh. It's like a face. It's a Rorschach mole!

CHRIS: We'll pay somebody to airbrush the stills.

LUCY: What if somebody from class sees it?

CHRIS: Who cares? You see them once a week.

LUCY: I see them once a week for four hours for another two and a half years.

CHRIS: After which you will never them again. You should be proud! You're putting a plan into action. They'll admire you for that.

LUCY: They'll think I'm a slut.

CHRIS: They'll think you're a slut because we post photos of you touching yourself online?

LUCY: Yes?

CHRIS: Strictly speaking isn't a slut someone who does it for free with many partners?

LUCY: Strictly speaking, yes.

CHRIS: Do you have many sexual partners I don't know about, from whom you receive no compensation?

LUCY: No.

CHRIS: Technically what we're going to do will make you more of a digital whore, or "ho" as the kids say. Not a slut.

LUCY: Goody.

CHRIS: This is a political statement! You're free to do as you please. This is freedom itself! Freedom's essence!

LUCY: Freedom to get naked on camera and beam it toward the infinite?

CHRIS: Freedom to get naked on camera and beam it toward the infinite!

LUCY: I'm freaking out!

CHRIS: Relax! If we stick to the plan, we'll be fine. It's a business! People love a woman who wants to share her beauty. You're like a Renaissance painter's muse, except in this case the Renaissance painter is anonymous. And everywhere all over the world. Forever.

LUCY: And using pictures of me to jerk off.

CHRIS: I thought we were past all this.

LUCY: All what?

CHRIS: You clearly need a trope to define yourself!
Here's one: think of yourself as the lovable stripper
who works one night a week to pay for college, or the
prostitute who goes to law/

LUCY: Don't call me a prostitute! You're on thin ice. I
can change my mind. I'm the one in control here!

CHRIS: Think about the money. Think about eating
steak and drinking nice wine somebody serves you.
Sure, maybe the service isn't great. But you know how
it is. She's been on her feet all day. She doesn't look
well. Oh, let's leave a nice tip. Twenty percent? You
know, waitresses work so hard. Poor thing. Probably
never went to college. Or worse, ha ha ha, she probably
got an English degree with a Gender Studies minor
and has all this debt she can't pay back and—

LUCY: Give me the camera.

(CHRIS *nearly hands the camera to* LUCY *but pulls back.*)

CHRIS: If you want to stop, now's the time. There's
always a day job. The chance to sell out and settle into
a routine. Hey, you'll get to decorate your very own
fuzzy box! Just one more cubicle for another drone in
the human herd! Smirking men in wool suits. Meeting
after meeting after meeting. Near tears all the time for
no discernable reason, because it's so damned obvious
life is slipping away. Tick tock. Tick tock. Pathetic
birthday cakes, and of course you have to sing and
mean it. Happy birthday to you! Happy birthday to
you!
Monday through Friday eight to five, repetitive days of
all that gray, gray, gray, gray nothing. Employee of the
month. Casual Fridays. You can wear jeans!

LUCY: (*Grabbing the camera*) Let's do it!

CHRIS: I love you. Hey. Look at me.

LUCY: Yeah yeah yeah.

(LUCY *goes to the computer in the living area and connects the camera to the laptop and prepares to send the photos.* CHRIS *follows and watches.*)

LUCY: Here we go. Let's press "send" together.

(CHRIS *and* LUCY *do.*)

LUCY: Those exist forever now.

CHRIS: Immortality.

LUCY: Sort of.

CHRIS: You're not horribly damaged.

LUCY: How do you know?

CHRIS: I live with you.

LUCY: I still have a few secrets.

CHRIS: Just wait until we open the web chat and stream video eight hours a day!

LUCY: It's going to be weird.

CHRIS: It's already weird. We live in a science fiction novel. Think about it. We'll be long gone, and people in the future will look back at us: all these flat, dead images from the past. Just so many zeros and ones. They'll have a special holiday for us. Digital Pioneers Day or something. They'll light virtual candles. The networks will observe a minute of silence, and we'll be/

LUCY: We need to hang that plant.

(*End Scene*)

Scene 3
MISTER TAKAYAMA'S AMERICA

(A month later. CHRIS *stands on a chair and waters the potted plant above the wireless router in the office. He fiddles with it a bit, organizing the leaves, then steps off the chair. He goes to the computer on the dining table and sits. He taps a few keys and stares at the screen.)*

*(*LUCY *enters.)*

CHRIS: Salve! How'd it go?

LUCY: Great! Prof took me aside and said I had a winner. He called it "personalized pornography featuring professional amateurs."

CHRIS: Everyone signs a non-compete, right?

LUCY: Of course. Listen, he said we need to—

CHRIS: Wait. Look! I have us linked up to every social networking website out there, adult and otherwise. There are like four hundred.
MeSpace. MeMeMe. I-I-I-Spot.
No, I have not developed a stutter. AdultChat YouSpot YouMeWe WeMeYou WeYouMe FaceDork DorkFace
I guess those are sites for dorks. The list goes on and on. We're linked up, so we're formally launched now. Here we are: AmericaInHeat.com. Your screen name is L-U-X-X-X. Luxxx. The girl next door! "The ultimate, innocent but somehow equally naughty expression of lusty, post-modern American sexual liberation and hedonistic decadence." Right from the plan. I mean we don't actually say that outright, but you get that impression from the pictures, the "About Me" section, everything. It's all about an image. The impression. It's semi…ugh, shit…why can't I talk right now?

LUCY: Semiotics.

CHRIS: Semiotics! The semiotics of pornography as it relates to new media and social networking.

LUCY: There's a subject for your thesis if you want to go back to college.

CHRIS: Fuck college. We're making money! All college ever did was force us to take out irresponsible loans. College is a pyramid scheme for the professors and the athletes. Here. You are "bi-curious but mostly straight, single, like to work out, do both Pilates and Yoga, and your dream is to one day be a lawyer." Your position on religion is "forgiving." I love that. It doesn't say you're a Christian but that's implied. Some kind of ethnic Christian, as if that was even a thing. Ha! And then people can imagine what they want. Oh, and you love anal.

LUCY: I love anal?

CHRIS: It's your favorite thing in the world.

LUCY: Am I going to have to do something about that?

CHRIS: Naturally. We're targeting an international market, and foreign guys want to give it to an American woman in the ass. Get us back for our savage cultural imperialism and Gitmo. It's basic psychology.

LUCY: I've always thought of it as an out hole.

CHRIS: I am aware. Oh oh oh! Look! You're already getting fan email. Some guy in Ontario wrote to say he can't wait to subscribe when the web chat is live. And see here? Our first paying subscriber!

LUCY: No way!

CHRIS: And we haven't even begun to stream video! Ten bucks. It's in the account!

LUCY: Oh my God!

CHRIS: Kiss this apartment goodbye! We're going to be able to buy some foreclosed ten bedroom monster. It's going to be great. We can buy like three houses. We'll be landlords. Lords of land! We will feast like suckling pigs upon the byproduct of the labor of others! We will finally be first class citizens. We'll get a foosball table!

LUCY: I so totally want a foosball table!

CHRIS: Look! We have this guy's information. His email address. We can tell when he's logged in and where from. We can see what pages he's visited. We even have his phone number.

LUCY: That is so cool.

CHRIS: He's Japanese. He's already spent like ten hours on the site. He's getting his money's worth. We might need to change our pricing model.

LUCY: What's he been doing on the site for ten hours?

CHRIS: He's visited a few times already.

LUCY: But there are just like what? Five pictures?

CHRIS: And your "blog".

LUCY: With three entries.

CHRIS: He must really like you.

LUCY: I guess.

CHRIS: He probably loves that you like anal. Or likes that you love it. What's the Japanese word for anal?

LUCY: Shut up!

CHRIS: Oh relax. He probably just leaves it up on the screen when he's away.

LUCY: I feel weird.

CHRIS: I bought champagne.
(He reveals champagne.)

LUCY: Umm. Hey. Guess who showed up in class today?

CHRIS: Who?

LUCY: Thompson.

CHRIS: What did he want?

LUCY: He joined the class. It's just a coincidence.

CHRIS: Or he's stalking you to get back at me for punching him! Revenge!

LUCY: He bit you. I'd say you're even.

CHRIS: Did he say anything?

LUCY: He said "hello." He's taking the class so he can move into a desk job. And he says you should call him sometime.

CHRIS: I'm not going to do that.

LUCY: Did you un-friend him?

CHRIS: Friend is not a verb!

LUCY: Why don't you tell me what actually happened?

CHRIS: What?

LUCY: You didn't punch Thompson for his laugh.

CHRIS: I don't want to talk about Thompson. I want to celebrate.

LUCY: Yeah, well. I have to deal with him now.

CHRIS: How'd his teeth look?

LUCY: Nice and straight.

CHRIS: If only he had something to sell. To AmericaInHeat.com and...Shenji Takayama.

LUCY: Cheers.

CHRIS: I really love you. I love Lucy.

LUCY: Yeah. The professor made one suggestion. We need to think about franchising. We need multiple revenue streams.

CHRIS: We're going to run ads.

LUCY: We want to be business owners, not self employed. So we need people willing to make themselves into products for the right amount of money. Franchisees.

CHRIS: Huh. Yeah. If it works once, it will work again. We sign somebody up to our network, do the set up for them, train them in, and take a percentage.

LUCY: That's the idea. I ran some numbers, and here's what we make annually if I'm a huge hit.

CHRIS: That's a nice number.

LUCY: Sure. But we can't bank on that. Most small businesses fail, and very few make a profit in the first couple of years. Now here's what we make if we just hit our target.

CHRIS: Respectable.

LUCY: Here's what we make if we hit half our target.

CHRIS: Not so good.

LUCY: Right? So how do we hedge against a bad year and make sure we don't end up without an income when my tits start to sag?

CHRIS: Implants?

LUCY: Shut up and look at this. Here's what we make if we bring in a hundred people who hit just half the target while we scrape a reasonable percentage from the top.

CHRIS: That's a lot of zeroes.

LUCY: Yes, dear, it is.

CHRIS: Huh. Yeah. Okay. But we should focus on you first. Prove that it works, right? I mean that's still the plan, isn't it?

LUCY: Sure. Listen though…

(The computer makes a sound.)

CHRIS: Shenji Takayama logged in!

LUCY: What time is it in Japan?

CHRIS: It's probably yesterday.

LUCY: Maybe it's tomorrow…

CHRIS & LUCY: Whoa.

LUCY: I still don't know. It's happening really fast.

CHRIS: Don't you think this is great? We'll finally be in charge of our own lives!

LUCY: Yeah… except, ugh. Here's the deal. Look.
(She types into the computer.)

CHRIS: What the hell is this? You didn't… What the fuck did you do?!

LUCY: Get over it, hypocrite. I'm all over the Internet and now you are too!

CHRIS: How do I delete this? What's the password? What's your password, Lucy?

LUCY: You're not thinking. You're reacting. Take a deep breath. Look at the screen. Scroll down.

CHRIS: This is a gay message board!

LUCY: Yes. It is a popular message board for homosexuals.

CHRIS: I didn't agree to this!

LUCY: A man from Japan is jerking off to photos of me as we speak.

CHRIS: Maybe he's reading your blog!

LUCY: Scroll down. There. See? You've got fans. And they want to be your friends! Look at all the messages. This guy wants you to wear panties. This guy wants you to jerk off on camera for…

CHRIS: How much?

LUCY: Fifty bucks. Not bad. Look at it this way: fifty bucks times ten thousand is—

CHRIS: Yeah yeah yeah. This guy wants my phone number. What the fuck is… Is that a human being?

LUCY: His name's Big Underscore Ben. He's from London.

CHRIS: That man is hairy.

LUCY: You know what else he is? A big fan. And his profile says he's in finance. Hmm. I bet he has ten dollars to spend. And friends who have ten dollars to spend!

CHRIS: What are you saying?

LUCY: I'm not going through with this unless you start a website too, Mister Feminist. Like you said: everything's for sale. Welcome to the new/

CHRIS: You can't expect me to—

LUCY: Oh shut up! You jobless deadbeat.

(LUCY *holds* CHRIS. *They hover over the computer.*)

LUCY: I love you, and because I love you, it's your turn now. You started a fire.

(*The computer makes another sound. Then another. Then another.* CHRIS *and* LUCY *stare at it. The lights fade until they are lighted only by the glow from the screen.*)

END OF ACT ONE

ACT TWO
[All Together Now]

Scene 1
RUBBER SOULS

(The apartment later that year. CHRIS *and* LUCY *have converted the living / dining room into opposite-facing faux-bedrooms. A pair of computers in the middle form a virtual "fourth wall". From the webcam at each computer one would get the impression one is peering into an actual bedroom. The hitherto office now doubles as a bedroom and an office. There is no longer a dining area. She sits at her computer in the office. He is on the edge of the bed in his faux-bedroom, a keyboard on his lap, fully dressed. They chat via their computers. For the handling of the [chat text in brackets] please refer to the note at the top of the script.)*

LUCY: [Who are you chatting with now?]

CHRIS: [Big_Ben.]

LUCY: [What's he want?]

CHRIS: [He wants me to stick a cucumber up my butt. He's got this thing with vegetables.]

LUCY: [ROFL]
(She is not.)

CHRIS: [It's not funny.]

LUCY: [Aww, poor baby.]

BIG_BEN: [Are you still there?]

CHRIXXX: [Yeah. I'm thinking about it.]

BIG_BEN: [Don't think too hard.]

CHRIXXX: [You make me so hot. I can't concentrate.]

BIG_BEN: [You make me so hot. You dirty Yank.]

CHRIXXX: [Thanks.]

BIG_BEN: [Say you're a dirty Yank.]

CHRIXXX: [I'm a dirty Yank.]

BIG_BEN: [You are. So nasty. So dirty. So? How about that cucumber?]

CHRIXXX: [I'm thinking about it.]

BIG_BEN: [You love your vegetables, don't you?]

CHRIXXX: [I do. I love cucumbers especially. I'm thinking about how big they are. I'm thinking specifically about circumference.]

BIG_BEN: [You're too smart for your own good, boy.]

CHRIXXX: [Yeah. I'm bad. I'm a bad Yankee Doodle.]

BIG_BEN: [A bad Yankee Doodle Dandy.]

CHRIXXX: [Bad bad bad.]

BIG_BEN: [Come on. I'll pay you in good solid English Pounds. Backed by the full authority of the English Crown.]

CHRIXXX: [How much?]

BIG_BEN: [You're a filthy colonial whore, aren't you?]

CHRIXXX: [I'm a filthy colonial whore. How much?]

BIG_BEN: [Eighty pounds.]

CHRIXXX: [You paid me eighty pounds for the carrot. You kept calling me Alice.]

BIG_BEN: [I remember. I was very late for an appointment, but I made time to watch you!]

CHRIXXX: [I want one hundred for a cucumber.]

BIG_BEN: [All right. A hundred. But I want the sound on this time. And I want you to call yourself Abraham Lincoln while you do it. Honest Abe. Honest and filthy. And I want you to pretend you lost the war.]

CHRIXXX: [The Civil War?]

BIG_BEN: [No, the War for Independence. Of course the Civil War! You're Abraham Lincoln.]

CHRIXXX: [Okay. That sounds hot. Let me see if we have a cucumber.]

BIG_BEN: [Mum always said a growing boy needs veg!]

CHRIXXX: [brb]

(CHRIS *turns off the webcam.*)

CHRIS: [Come here.]

LUCY: [You come here.]

CHRIS: [I'm working.]

LUCY: [No you're not. You're chatting with me.]

CHRIS: [What are you doing?]

LUCY: [Looking at pictures of the house.]

CHRIS: [Have they had an offer yet?]

LUCY: [Nobody's buying.]

CHRIS: [That's great.]

LUCY: [Not for the sellers. Poor bastards.]

CHRIS: [Their loss is our gain.]

LUCY: [Spoken like a true capitalist.]

CHRIS: [When in Rome.]

LUCY: [So, Chrixxx…are you going to stick a cucumber up your butt for Big_Ben?]

CHRIS: (*Yelling*) Ahhh! We're doing it again!

LUCY: *(Yelling)* I know!

CHRIS: We're deranged!

LUCY: We are not deranged!

CHRIS: Our thoughts are being beamed around the globe and back into the next room!

LUCY: What?!

CHRIS: Never mind! Do we have any cucumbers!?

LUCY: *(From the doorway)* How much did he offer?

CHRIS: A hundred pounds. He said eighty but I talked him up.

LUCY: Negotiation! You're becoming a real entrepreneur. A cucumber up the butt is definitely worth more than a carrot.

CHRIS: I'm on the fence. He wants to use sound too this time. He wants me to call myself Abraham Lincoln and pretend I lost the Civil War.

LUCY: You can do that.

(CHRIS takes off his pants, revealing colorful underwear. He changes into something "sexy" in preparation for his session.)

CHRIS: It's kind of weird, isn't it?

LUCY: Who cares? We sell fantasy. A hundred pounds isn't bad for a cucumber up the butt. The Pound's really strong.

CHRIS: Do we even have a cucumber?

LUCY: A couple. Just pick the smallest one. You want me to lube you up?

CHRIS: You bitch. You love this.

LUCY: Better not keep Big Underscore Ben waiting.

CHRIS: How much are they asking for the house?

LUCY: Here.

CHRIS: That's cheap! What did they pay for it?

LUCY: Twice that.

CHRIS: That's an apocalyptic collapse in value! And that's just one property. We shouldn't buy a house. We should buy crossbows and a water purifier.

LUCY: Oh come on. It's the market correcting itself. No need to get weird. We just need ten percent down.

CHRIS: How many hits did we get last week?

(LUCY *struts toward* CHRIS *and stands in front of him.*)

LUCY: A lot.

CHRIS: How many new subscribers?

LUCY: A lot a lot.

CHRIS: How many?

LUCY: A lot like…this. And this. And…

(CHRIS *and* LUCY *kiss. She grabs his crotch.*)

LUCY: And this especially.

CHRIS: Ungh. Ahh. Umm. That many?!

LUCY: Ugh huh.

CHRIS: That's good. That's really good.

LUCY: But we have to keep going. That's how this works. You find a gimmick and exploit it.

CHRIS: Sex isn't a gimmick.

LUCY: Sex is the ultimate gimmick.
(*She snaps the band of his underwear.*)
Save it for your clients.

CHRIS: Ugh. Go get me a cucumber. Please?

(LUCY *exits and returns with an exceptionally long cucumber.*)

LUCY: It's the smallest one we have.

CHRIS: You're kidding me.

LUCY: You want me to get the other one? I checked. This one's long but it's not as round.

CHRIS: Get the other one.

(LUCY *exits and returns with a very round cucumber.*)

LUCY: I was going to make a salad, but a hundred pounds buys a lot of salad, so... long or thick? What do you prefer? It's an ancient dilemma, really. Women have dealt with it since the dawn of time. Men too really.

CHRIS: Give me the long one.

LUCY: Ahh. The classical choice. I prefer a bit of both, myself. But you knew that. You can always say no.

CHRIS: We haven't said no yet, and I don't want to start now.

LUCY: Good. Here you go. The best lubricant Federal Reserve Notes can buy. Long or thick you aren't going to stick it up there dry.

CHRIS: Don't watch. Please?

(LUCY *exits with her laptop.* CHRIS *sits at his computer. He holds the lube in one hand and the cucumber in the other.*)

LUCY: [I love you.]

CHRIS: [I know you do.]

LUCY: [You okay?]

CHRIS: [Yeah. Just stay in the other room.]

LUCY: [ok]

CHRIS: [It's like I never have enough time. You can't not play the game.]

BIG_BEN: [Tick tock. Hey, Yankee Doodle. Are you still there?]

LUCY: [We just need to get better at the game. That's all. Then we'll have more time and space and… freedom. We'll buy some freedom. What else can we do?]

CHRIS: [I feel invisible most of the time.]

LUCY: [That's not true. I see you. I see you, and I love you.]

BIG_BEN: [Hello! Yankee Dooooooooooodle!!!]

CHRIXXX: [I'm still here.]

BIG_BEN: [I can't see you. Turn on the camera.]

CHRIXXX: [One sec]

CHRIS: [But that's the point. You can't see me. You're in the next room.]

LUCY: [You know what I mean.]

CHRIS: [Some days I don't even feel human. I feel like I've fallen out of something beautiful and old and true. Like when I was a kid I could run around all day and I'd feel… I don't know.]

BIG_BEN: [Tick tock. Tick tock. Tick tock.]

CHRIS: [He's so pushy.]

LUCY: [He's the client. He gets to be pushy. You better go.]

CHRIS: [Yeah. Later.]

LUCY: [I love you.]
I! Love! You!

(CHRIS *turns on his webcam.*)

BIG_BEN: [Aha! There you are.]

CHRIXXX: [Here I am.]

BIG_BEN: [Say something.]

CHRIS: Something.

Big_Ben: [I can't hear you. What did you say?]

Chrixxx: [Something.]

Big_Ben: [Clever boy. I had my speakers muted. Try again. Say something smart. And sexy.]

Chris: *(From a notebook, slowly making it "sexy")* Liberal democracy as the political supplement of the global capitalist hegemony serves to mollify the so-called "middle" classes and subvert the revolutionary tendencies of the so-called "working" classes. Its principal agents are the corporate media and the military industrial complex.

Big_Ben: [Stop stop stop! What's with the lefty nonsense? You are a bad Yankee Doodle. It's boring. And it turns me OFF!!! Well? Say something nice.]

Chris: Hey, Ben. Can I call you Ben?

Big_Ben: [Sure.]

Chris: You can talk to me if you want. With your real voice I mean. You have a microphone?

Big_Ben: [I'm just going to type. I don't like the sound of my voice.]

Chris: Okay. Umm.

Big_Ben: [Did you get the cucumber?]

Chris: Yep. Here she is.

Big_Ben: [Turn it all around for me. Hmm. Is that the widest one you've got?]

Chris: Yes.

Big_Ben: [I suppose it will have to do. What's his name?]

Chris: It's a he?

Big_Ben: [Of course it's a he.]

Chris: What do you want me to call him?

BIG_BEN: [Let's call him Karl with a K.]

CHRIS: Okay. Well Karl with a K and I are going on a little date. Isn't that right, Karl?
(*As Karl the cucumber*)
That's right, Chrixxx!

BIG_BEN: [Yes. Good. But your name is Abe.]

CHRIS: (*As Karl the Cucumber*) That's right, Abe! And you've been bad! You lost the Civil War!

BIG_BEN: [Say, "The South has risen!"]

CHRIS: The South has risen!

BIG_BEN: [Karl says that!]

CHRIS: (*As Karl the Cucumber*) The South has risen! How's that?

BIG_BEN: [Great.]

CHRIS: We said a hundred pounds, right?

BIG_BEN: [You should see it in your account.]

CHRIS: I see it. Thanks.

BIG_BEN: [No, thank you. I'm going to play you some good old-fashioned English music while you do it. You like good old-fashioned English music, don't you?]

CHRIS: Sure.

(*Indistinct music trickles through the computer. It sounds familiar, but something's wrong with it.*)

CHRIS: What is that?

BIG_BEN: [It's the Beatles. You don't like the Beatles?]

CHRIS: No. I love the Beatles. It just doesn't sound right.

BIG_BEN: [It sounds great on my end.]

CHRIS: Does it have to be the Beatles?

BIG_BEN: [Yes, Mister President. It does.]

CHRIS: Okay. Well. Why don't you tell me what you want me to do?

BIG_BEN: [All right, Honest Abe. First let me see how nice you can be to Karl. Be nice. Pet him. Stroke Karl. All the way up and down.]

CHRIS: How's this?

BIG_BEN: [Oh yes, that's good. You have nice hands.]

(LUCY *quietly moves so she can watch* CHRIS. *He does not see her.*)

CHRIS: Thank you.

BIG_BEN: [Mmm. Karl wants to touch your nips.]

(LUCY *sneaks into view and watches.*)

CHRIS: My what?

BIG_BEN: [You know damn well what I mean! You're an educated man, Mister President. A lawyer! An autodidact! Candlelight. Log cabin. I'm English and even I know the story! Come on now. Let Karl touch the First Nipples.]

CHRIS: It's cold.

BIG_BEN: [Now give Karl a nice kiss. No no no, a real kiss!!! There you go. See, that's nice. Even veg needs love. Lick him. Lick. Good! Lick lick lick. You know the tongue is the strongest muscle in the human body?]

CHRIS: Ungh huh.

BIG_BEN: [Now put him in your mouth.]

CHRIS: Isn't he going in my ass?

BIG_BEN: [First the mouth!]

CHRIS: I've got lube if that's what you're—

BIG_BEN: [I WANT TO SEE YOU PUT KARL THE CUCUMBER IN YOUR MOUTH, OKAY?! I'M

PAYING YOU, AREN'T I!? NOW DO WHAT I
WANT!!!!!]

CHRIS: All right! You don't need the caps lock!

BIG_BEN: [I was using the shift key. Now put Karl in
your mouth. There you go. Perfect. Open wide, Mister
President. Wide. Wider! WIDER!!!!!!]

(LUCY *stares, rapt. She touches herself and gasps.* CHRIS
*sees her and pulls the cucumber out of his mouth. They stare
at one another a moment.*)

(*End Scene*)

Scene 2
REVOLVER

(*The apartment. The plant has begun to wither.* CHRIS *and*
LUCY *have not noticed.* CHRIS *has just wrapped up a session
with a client and looks at photos of* LUCY. LUCY *deals with a
client:* TOMMYKNOCKER.)

TOMMYKNOCKER: [Knock knock knock.]

LUXXX: [Well hello there. What's your name?]

TOMMYKNOCKER: [I'm Tommyknocker. From Canada.]

LUXXX: [Hi there, Tommyknocker from Canada.]

TOMMYKNOCKER: [You look so hot.]

LUXXX: [Thanks. So, why don't you tell me what you
want?]

TOMMYKNOCKER: [I just want to look at you.]

LUXXX: [Are you sure? Don't you want me to do
anything in particular?]

TOMMYKNOCKER: [I like you like this. I just want to
look.]

LUXXX: [Okay. Just like this, huh?]

TOMMYKNOCKER: [Yeah. Perfect.]

LUXXX: [lol]

(LUCY *isn't*.)

TOMMYKNOCKER: [Are you laughing at me?]

LUXXX: [No. I just think you're cute.]

TOMMYKNOCKER: [Cute?]

LUXXX: [You're paying me just to sit here. And type. It's cute.]

TOMMYKNOCKER: [You're cute. You're HOT.]

LUXXX: [Thanks.]

TOMMYKNOCKER: [I want to hear your voice. Turn on your microphone.]

LUXXX: [Oh I'm sorry. My microphone isn't working right now! Is that okay?]

CHRIS: [What's going on?]

LUCY: [Some guy is paying just to chat. And look.]

CHRIS: [Nice!]

LUXXX: [Hello. Are you still there?]

(*TOMMYKNOCKER has signed off.*)

LUCY: [He just signed off. Wow. Talk about easy money.]

CHRIS: [You're beautiful. I could look at you all day.]

LUCY: [Focus on your clients.]

CHRIS: [I can't help it. You distract me.]

LUCY: [We need more space. We have to be able to use sound whenever we need it. That's what clients expect. I don't like lying to them. Telling them my microphone isn't working. It makes me feel cheap.]

CHRIS: [I want to make love to you right now.]

LUCY: [We can't. We have to save it.]

CHRIS: [I know.]

LUCY: [Once we've established ourselves we can take a break. Then we can go at it like bunnies.]

CHRIS: [I really want to go at it like bunnies.]

LUCY: [Me too. But we need to have discipline. Like sexual samurai. Who's my sexual samurai?]

CHRIS: [I am.]

LUCY: [Say it like you mean it.]

CHRIS: [I AM, SENSEI!]

LUCY: [That's better. I want a drink. You want one?]

CHRIS: [A drink drink or just a drink?]

LUCY: [I'll have a drink drink if you'll have a drink drink.]

CHRIS: [I earned it. I'm exhausted.]

LUCY: [You're getting good with vegetables.]

CHRIS: [Ha ha ha. Bitch.]

(CHRIS *flips* LUCY *off "in reality." She returns the gesture, stands, and brings back two drinks. She hands one to him. They drink. They sit again at their laptops.)*

CHRIS: [How's Takayama-san?]

LUCY: [He's learned some English. He's beyond emoticons. He wrote 'Tank you' tonight.]

CHRIS: [Tank you?]

LUCY: [Yeah. Tank you.]

CHRIS: [You're a tank-operator!]

LUCY: [lol]
(She isn't.)

CHRIS: [Why don't we make an offer on that house?]

LUCY: Really?

CHRIS: [Really.]

LUCY: Here! Right here.

CHRIS: [Sure. We can afford it.]

LUCY: Chris!

CHRIS: Ahh! Sorry. Yeah, we should. Make an offer. Let's do it. I'll email the realtor.

LUCY: Are you sure?

CHRIS: We need to expand.

LUCY: What if we get burned? Five years ago that house was worth twice as much.

CHRIS: It can't get any worse, can it? And if it does at least we'll have a house. We can start a family. Run the business. It's like eight bedrooms if you count the basement!

LUCY: You still want to start a family?

CHRIS: You don't?

LUCY: Maybe. Later. I'm in my prime here. If I get pregnant, I won't be able to work.

CHRIS: Says who?

LUCY: Seriously?

CHRIS: Same business, different market.

LUCY: Wow. Huh. I don't know about that…

CHRIS: But you want the house, right?

LUCY: Yes. Absolutely. Let's do it.

CHRIS: We don't have the whole down payment.

LUCY: We need the space. Come on. We can afford it. We're alchemists now! Our butts turn vegetables into gold.

CHRIS: Let's do it.

LUCY: I'm excited!

CHRIS: Let's toast. To AmericaInHeat.com and the insatiable voyeurism of our clients!

LUCY: Yay!

CHRIS: I'll email the realtor.

(CHRIS *and* LUCY *return to their terminals. He begins typing.*)

BIG_BEN: [Yankee Doodle!!! What time is it there? I'm horny.]

CHRIS: It's Big Underscore Ben again. And he's horny.

LUCY: That guy has two settings: horny and asleep.

CHRIXXX: [I'm going to bed soon.]

BIG_BEN: [I've been up all night PARTYING. WOOOOOO!!!]

CHRIS: I should chat with him.

LUCY: Tell him it's late and you want to go to bed.

CHRIS: He's my best client!

BIG_BEN: [I'm here with friends. They want to see you do something freaky.]

CHRIS: He says he's with friends and wants to see me do something freaky.

LUCY: Freakier than a cucumber up the butt?

CHRIS: I guess.

LUCY: Maybe a squash! Go on. Ask him.

CHRIXXX: [Like what?]

BIG_BEN: [Five hundred pounds to drink your own piss.]

CHRIXXX: [I've never done that.]

BIG_BEN: [First time for everything. Come on. Five hundred pounds. I know you need it.]

CHRIS: Wow. Five hundred pounds to drink my own piss.

LUCY: Really? That's disgusting. And lucrative!
(*She comes around the computer and stands in front of the monitor.*)

BIG_BEN: [Who is that?]

CHRIS: Damn it, Lucy! The camera's on!

LUCY: Turn it off!

(CHRIS *turns off the camera.*)

BIG_BEN: [You have a friend there I don't know about?]

CHRIXXX: [It's nobody.]

LUCY: Never leave the camera on!

CHRIS: I forgot!

BIG_BEN: [You got a woman there, Chrixxx?]

CHRIS: What do I tell him?

LUCY: I don't know!

BIG_BEN: [Tick tock! Tick Tock! Tick tock!]

CHRIXXX: [She's just a friend.]

BIG_BEN: [Hold on. My friends and I are talking here.]

LUCY: Is it off now?

CHRIS: Yeah, it's off.

(LUCY *comes around to look at the chat.*)

BIG_BEN: [Was that your girlfriend, Yankee Doodle?]

LUCY: Don't tell him anything.

CHRIS: I'm not going to lie.

LUCY: Whatever. He's your client.

CHRIXXX: [She's my girlfriend.]

BIG_BEN: [I didn't know you go both ways!]

CHRIXXX: [Well I do.]

BIG_BEN: [That's not what your profile says.]

CHRIXXX: [I still have a few secrets.]

BIG_BEN: [Does she live with you?]

CHRIXXX: [Yes.]

LUCY: This is so messed up.

BIG_BEN: [Do you love her?]

CHRIXXX: [Very much.]

LUCY: Stop telling him about our lives!

BIG_BEN: [Does she let you in the back door? Come on, boy! You can tell me!]

CHRIXXX: [I'm not telling you that.]

BIG_BEN: [We'll pay you a thousand pounds to have her in the arse right now. We're having a PARTY!!! We want to WATCH!!!]

LUCY: Is he serious?

CHRIS: The dude's loaded.

BIG_BEN: [Turn on the camera. Come on!!!]

CHRIS: He wants me to turn on the camera.

LUCY: Turn it on.

(CHRIS *turns on the camera.*)

CHRIS: We can still say no.

LUCY: I do anal for my clients.

CHRIS: That's different.

LUCY: If we start telling people no, it'll hurt the business. We promised each other.

CHRIS: Okay…

LUCY: Let's try and talk him up.

BIG_BEN: [Tick tock! Come on, Yankee Doodle.]

(LUCY *takes* CHRIS' *keyboard and appears on the webcam again. She types into his chat window.*)

CHRIXXX: [We want two thousand.]

BIG_BEN: [Hey! She's back. Hello. What's your name?]

CHRIXXX: [Luxxx.]

BIG_BEN: [Well, Luxxx. How about it?]

CHRIXXX: [We want two thousand. You can watch us all night.]

BIG_BEN: [Two thousand pounds? Let me check with my friends. My friends say sure. Why not? It's been a good year. Turn on your microphone. We want to listen!]

CHRIS: Can you hear me?

BIG_BEN: [Yes. Good. We'll play you some music!]

(*The sound of strange, tinny music comes through the computer along with the insect din of a waning party. The song becomes clear: Yankee Doodle.*)

CHRIS: What the hell is that?

BIG_BEN: [Music! We're having a PARTY!!! This is what an English party sounds like. Come on, Yankee Doodle. We don't have all day. Some of us actually work for a living. Ha ha ha ha ha.]

CHRIS: Are you sure?

LUCY: It's a lot of money! We need it for the down payment. Come on. Come on! What? It's just sex.

CHRIS: This isn't the same. It's not just sex anymore… this is different. This is something—

(LUCY *pulls* CHRIS *onto the bed.*)

(*End Scene*)

Scene 3
LUCY IN THE SKY

(A month later. The hanging plant is dead. LUCY *and* CHRIS
sit at their laptops.)

LUCY: It's been what? A month?

CHRIS: Yeah.

LUCY: He's not coming back, is he?

CHRIS: We should have gotten the money first.

LUCY: I got carried away.

CHRIS: I guess.

LUCY: Lesson learned, right?

CHRIS: He was my best client.

LUCY: We sell illusion. It's fragile.

CHRIS: Everything's fragile.

LUCY: Oh shush. Moving guys come tomorrow. And
then we'll start franchising. That's where the real
money is.

CHRIS: I'm going to shower. You want to join me?

LUCY: I have another session.

CHRIS: Takayama-san?

LUCY: Tommyknocker? From Canada? He's the guy
who just likes to chat.

CHRIS: As long as he pays.

LUCY: He pays.

CHRIS: You know we've ceased to be human, don't
you?

LUCY: Oh shut up.

CHRIS: You feel like you're connected, but you're
actually /

LUCY: You and I have more money than we've ever had in our lives. Real money. Not ideas. Not good intentions. You can't eat good intentions. Hate to break it to you.

CHRIS: But we have changed, and now there's no way back! Pandora's box. Once it's opened, you can't go back to the way—

LUCY: Would you shut up?

CHRIS: We aren't even—

LUCY: Chris! You aren't thinking clearly. You crammed half the produce section up your ass this week. Go take a bath. You smell like a salad bar.

CHRIS: Yeah. All right. Vale.

LUCY: Vale right back, dork. Hey. Trust me. We're going to be rich. Then you can philosophize to your heart's content.

CHRIS: My heart stopped talking a long time ago.

LUCY: Oh go take a bath. Rub yourself with some vinaigrette. You'll feel better.

(CHRIS *exits.*)

TOMMYKNOCKER: [Knock knock knock. Hey, are you there?]

LUXXX: [Hello.]

TOMMYKNOCKER: [I have something for you.]

LUXXX: [For me?]

TOMMYKNOCKER: [Yes.]

LUXXX: [That's sweet of you. What is it?]

(*There are knocks at the door.*)

LUCY: Chris! Somebody's at the door!

TOMMYKNOCKER: [Are you still there?]

LUXXX: [brb]

TOMMYKNOCKER: [Don't take too long.]

(LUCY *goes to the front door. She opens it. There is a small present. She returns to her laptop and sits holding the present.*)

TOMMYKNOCKER: [Do you like it?]

LUXXX: [Who are you?]

TOMMYKNOCKER: [I got you a present.]

LUXXX: [Who the fuck are you? How'd you get our address?]

TOMMYKNOCKER: [You know me. I'm Tommyknocker. From Canada. Knock knock knock. Come on. Open the present.]

LUXXX: [No way. You're a creep.]

LUCY: Chris! Chris! Hey. Get in here!

CHRIS: (*Entering in a robe*) What? What's that?

LUCY: Look. Here.

TOMMYKNOCKER: [It's not polite to refuse gifts.]

(LUCY's *webcam turns on.*)

CHRIS: Who the hell is this guy?

LUCY: Tommyknocker!

(CHRIS *types at* LUCY's *keyboard.*)

TOMMYKNOCKER: [I'm a paying customer. I want a show, baby!!!]

CHRIS: This dude's not from Canada.

LUCY: It says he's from Canada!

CHRIS: His profile says he's from Canada. His I P says he's from…here.

LUCY: It has to be Thompson.

TOMMYKNOCKER: [I see you! Why don't you put some clothes on? Dirty bitch! Who's your friend there?]

LUCY: The camera's on!

CHRIS: Did you turn it on?

LUCY: No!

CHRIS: Somebody hacked your computer.

LUXXX: [CREEP!!!]

TOMMYKNOCKER: [That's no way to treat a paying CUSTOMER!]

CHRIS: It has to be Thompson. That dirty son of a bitch.

TOMMYKNOCKER: [Thomson? Who's Thomson? I don't know a Thomson!]

LUCY: He can hear us!

(CHRIS *goes to the router. He pulls down the hanging plant.*)

LUCY: What kind of freak sends somebody he meets on the Internet a present? You think I like you? You're just another loser creep. You're nobody! You aren't even fucking real! I can turn you off whenever I want! You fucking loser/

TOMMYKNOCKER: [No. Don't say that! I'm your #1 fan. I LIKE YOU! I THOUGHT WE WERE FRIENDS! YOU'RE MY ONLINE GIRLFRIEND!!!!!!]

(CHRIS *smashes the hanging plant into the router. He smashes the router again and again with the plant.*)

TOMMYKNOCKER: [DON'T YOU LIKE ME TOO!!?!? AREN'T YOU MY FRIEND!?!!! DON'T YOU WANT TO KNOW WHAT'S IN THE PRESENT? DON'T YOU WANT]

(CHRIS *stands over the destroyed router.* LUCY *stands clutching the present.*)

(*End Scene*)

Epilogue
All You Need Is [Like]

(CHRIS and LUCY's starter mansion. She is up front on a laptop. She wears a cute little golf hat. A putter leans on a table nearby. He is way off to the side.)

LUCY: [Did you talk to our lawyers?]

CHRIS: [We're hidden behind two layers of incorporation. Thompson or whoever won't find us.]

LUCY: [Nice.]

CHRIS: [Ahh! We're doing it again.]

LUCY: [Who cares? We're on opposite sides of a huge house! I bet you can't even hear me if I yell.]
You can't hear me, can you!? [Did you hear me?]

CHRIS: [It sounded like a dog barking.]

LUCY: [See.]

CHRIS: [What are they doing?]

LUCY: [Watching me. Waiting.]

CHRIS: [Good. Make them sweat a little.]

LUCY: [Let's not be cruel now.]

CHRIS: [It's just business, right?]

LUCY: [lol]
(She actually laughs this time, only too much. It is a terrible laugh, like somebody on serious drugs during severe airplane turbulence.)
Ahh hah. Ha. Hoooo. Excuse me. I just…oh me. Well hello, everybody. I'm so glad you could come. Let me just turn this on here. You have to get used to being on camera if you want to work with us!
(She turns on a camera and directs it at the audience.)
All right. We'll get started just as soon as my partner gets here!

(Typing as she speaks)

[We'll get started just as soon as my partner gets here!]

CHRIS: [How do they look?]

LUCY: [Come see for yourself.]

CHRIS: [I'm not sure anymore, Lucy.]

LUCY: [What's the problem?]

CHRIS: [Do you remember that present?]

LUCY: [From the creep? What does that have to do with anything?]

CHRIS: [I've got it right here.]

LUCY: I'm so sorry. Something just came up. Things go a mile a minute here at AmericaInHeat.com. So much technology!
[You said you threw it out.]

CHRIS: [I lied.]

LUCY: [Why?!]

CHRIS: [I don't know what we're doing. This thing is really big, and I don't feel like it's...]

LUCY: [Like it's what? Ethical? Get over it!]

CHRIS: [I'm just not sure anymore.]

LUCY: [It was your idea! And it's turned out great! We're going to be rich. This is what you wanted. Freedom! Hey. Hey! Are you still there?]

CHRIS: [Yeah.]

LUCY: [Just throw the present away and forget about it!]

CHRIS: [I'm going to open it.]

LUCY: [It might be dangerous!]

CHRIS: [It's probably just a love letter or something.]

LUCY: [Is that what you've been doing all day? Sitting up there with that stupid box?]

CHRIS: [Yes.]

LUCY: [Why?!]

CHRIS: [I'm curious. Aren't you curious?]

LUCY: [No! I don't give a damn about some box. Just get down here.]

CHRIS: [I'm not coming. You go ahead. Do it without me.]

LUCY: [You're not behaving like a professional. Would you get down here and join the rest of us in reality? Please? Chris? Come on. They're waiting! Hey! Chris! Chris! Goddamn it don't you dare sign off!]

(CHRIS closes his laptop and sets it aside. He holds the present. He shakes it gently. He sniffs it. He puts his ear up to it. He sets it down and stares.)

LUCY: We're so excited to tell you about AmericaInHeat.com and how you can be a part of it. It's so much better than working for the man! I was a waitress not all that long ago. Boy am I glad that phase of my life is over!
(She takes up the golf putter and holds it. She glances at her laptop and then looks to the audience.)
Well, friends, looks like my partner is dealing with a little technical hiccup. You know how that goes! So why don't we just get started? You probably have a bunch of questions about things like health insurance, dental, 401k, eck cetera, and I promise we'll get to those. But first I'd like to tell you exactly what it is we do here. As you read in our advertisement, we are an erotic services company. Have no illusions. Our corporate philosophy is to be forthright and transparent with both our clients and potential franchisees.

To be clear: we do not sell sex. We sell the idea of sex.
And an idea, unlike mere flesh, can be perfect. You see,
we have discovered that most people want something
they can't touch or smell or taste. They want perfection.
And they want control. And that's what we offer: the
perfect illusion of control.

It's just another game. In fact I like to think of this
business like I think of my favorite sport: golf. You can
always work on a part of your game.

(LUCY *makes a little show of swinging the putter. She smiles
and sets the putter aside.* CHRIS *takes a hit of vodka, pounds
a beer, and puts his hands on the present.*)

LUCY: Now I have to be blunt. Not all of you are cut
out for this. Even those of you who have the qualities
we're looking for just might not be a good fit. We
might not need another one of your type, or you might
not be willing to do the things you'll have to do to
succeed.

Sometimes our clients make strange requests, and our
policy is to say yes whenever possible. Bottom line:
there will be a high rate of attrition among even those
of you who do join us.

It's like that in any serious business, and I don't want
you to think if you fail that it's anything personal. It's
not. This is strictly business.

(CHRIS *begins to open the present. He plays with the
wrapping. He tugs at the bow a bit.*)

LUCY: Now that's out of the way, let's have some fun!
Let's find some common ground. I have a question for
you. Show of hands now! How many of you have ever
gone online for sex? I don't mean directly to solicit sex,
although that's fine too. How many have gone on just
to date? Anyone?

(*She ad libs to responses as they come.*)

You can admit it. It's nothing to be ashamed of.
Everybody does it! It's the twenty-first century! At
AmericaInHeat.com we like to say that today is
tomorrow, and tomorrow is yesterday. So why not live
for today?

(The light dims such that LUCY *is lighted only by the glow
from her laptop. She closes the laptop. Just as She does,*
CHRIS *opens the present. He stares into it. It glows with a
flickering light.)*

LUCY: Come on now. Don't be shy. We're all friends
here.

*(*CHRIS *reaches into the box with his hand and)*

END OF PLAY

* 9 7 8 0 8 8 1 4 5 8 9 9 2 *